How Big Is Our Baby?

Kane Miller
A DIVISION OF EDC PUBLISHING

First American Edition 2019
Kane Miller, A Division of EDC Publishing

Text copyright © Smriti Prasadam-Halls, 2019
Illustration copyright © Britta Teckentrup, 2019
The moral rights of the author and illustrator have been asserted.

First published in Great Britain in 2019 by Wren & Rook, an imprint of
Hachette Children's Group, part of Hodder & Stoughton

Library of Congress Control Number: 2018958211

Printed and bound in China
1 2 3 4 5 6 7 8 9 10
ISBN: 978-1-61067-953-4

For the bouncy babies
and the big brothers and sisters
who love them – S.P–H.

For Irina – B.T.

smriti prasadam-halls • britta teckentrup

How
Big
Is Our
Baby?

Congratulations!

You're going to have a baby **brother** or **sister**.

That means you're going to be a **big** brother or sister soon!

This little person will be a brand-new
friend to play with. You're going to be
a **very** important part of their life.

After all, they're going to
need someone to teach
them lots of clever things
as they grow up ...
and that's **you**!

After hearing such big news, you're
bound to have lots of feelings.

Happy!

Curious!

Impatient!

It's **wonderful** news,
so make sure you celebrate.

You may also feel a little worried. Soon you're going to be sharing your family, your toys and your home with a new someone.

If you're worrying that life will never be the same, you're right – it won't be. It's going to be even better!

There's going to be **MORE** fun, **MORE** cuddles and **MORE** love.

Everything needs time and a safe place to grow.

After all, flowers grow in rich soil.

And cupcakes rise in a warm oven.

A baby is just the same. It needs to live somewhere safe and warm while it develops and gets strong. That's a special place inside your mom called the **womb**.

Pregnancy is the name we give to the nine months that the baby spends in the womb. There, the baby is fed and protected as it gets bigger and bigger, until it is ready to come out and meet you.

Let's explore how Baby is going to develop during pregnancy!

month

Baby is as small as a speck of **sand** at the seaside.

Baby is **tiny**!

A special code for Baby is already in place. It's like a unique **recipe** that comes from both parents, and controls things like hair color, eye color and skin tone.

Soon this little someone will have **eyes**, **ears**, a **nose** and a **mouth**.

What color are your eyes?

2

months

Baby is the size of a **jelly bean**.

Baby may still be small, but the most important parts of its body are in place. The **heart** pumps blood, the **brain** thinks and the **lungs** will help Baby breathe.

Our little one has a heartbeat! It's too gentle to feel at the moment, though.

Believe it or not, Baby has a tiny **tail** and **webbed feet**. Don't worry, they'll disappear soon.

Put your hand over your heart and see if you can feel your own heartbeat. It helps if you do five jumping jacks first!

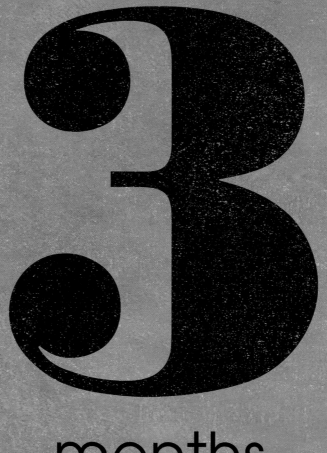

3

months

Baby is the size of an **egg**.

While growing in the womb, Baby is known as a **fetus**.

The tiny tot has **fingers** and **toes**, just like you.

How many fingers and toes do you have?

Baby gets at least twice as heavy during this month. Just imagine if you doubled your weight in four weeks!

4 months

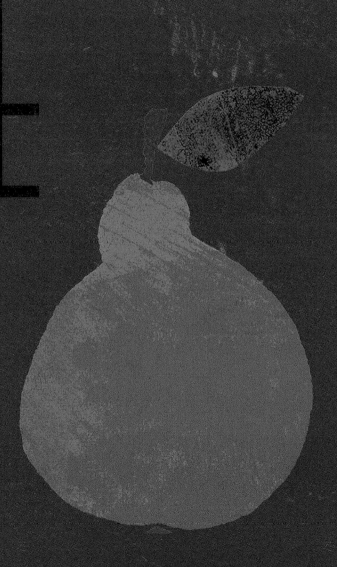

Baby is the size of a **pear**.

This month, you may be able to discover if Baby is a **boy** or a **girl**. Some families like to find out, and others prefer to have a surprise when Baby is born.

The little one is growing **eyebrows** and **hair**.

Baby can start making finger movements.

Wriggle your fingers and wave to Baby!

5 months

Baby is the size of a **mango**.

Baby can hear **sounds** now.

Sing a song
so the little one can
get to know
your voice!

Baby is wiggling
and jiggling all
around.

Your mom might feel Baby **move** for
the very first time. It's a fluttery feeling
in the womb – imagine if a butterfly
was inside your tummy!

6 months

Baby is the size of an **eggplant**.

7 months

Baby is the size of a **cauliflower**.

Baby might be doing some really big **kicks**.

Ask if you can feel them. Perhaps Baby is going to be a soccer player or a dancer!

Baby is getting bigger and stronger from the good food your mom is eating. A special **cord** passes food between her and the little one.

Baby is also growing little **eyelashes**.

8 months

months

Baby is the size of a **soccer ball**.

Baby is now probably upside down in your mom's womb, getting into position to be born. Can you imagine being on your head all day?

Baby can sleep and dream, just like you!

Baby sleeps and wakes at different times each day and night.

What do you think Baby is doing right now?

9 months

Baby is the size of a **watermelon**.

Baby is so **big**. Imagine carrying a heavy watermelon around with you all day! Can you think of some ways to help your mom when she's feeling tired?

The little one can **blink**, **cry**, **sleep** and **smile** ... even **suck** their **thumb**.

Thumbs up little Baby, you're ready to be born!

When Baby comes

Usually Baby decides
when to arrive, but
sometimes the **birth**
of a baby is planned
for a particular day.

Some babies
are born in the
hospital and some
are born at **home**.

It's hard work bringing a brand-new person
into the world. Your mom might be a little
worn out at first.

**She will
need lots
of rest!**

Wherever and whenever Baby arrives, he or she is going
to be **excited** to meet you. Be ready to give Baby
a lovely, big, warm **welcome** into your family!

To begin with, it may seem like Baby does a great deal of **sleeping, crying** and **feeding**! But it's all really important if Baby is going to grow into a healthy, strong person. Your parents might not be able to play as much as usual while they're looking after the little one – but that doesn't mean they don't want to play at all.

Why don't you bring some books to them while they're feeding Baby, or show everyone some of your drawings?

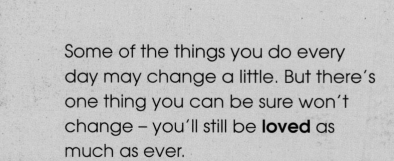

Some of the things you do every day may change a little. But there's one thing you can be sure won't change – you'll still be **loved** as much as ever.

You may have lots of good ideas about how to help with Baby. Your family will love to hear your suggestions – just make sure to ask first before you do anything.

Baby will love it if you **talk**, **sing songs** and make **funny faces**. Babies love to laugh!

Don't forget to add in plenty of cuddles and kisses.

Your most important job is to enjoy getting to know Baby. Because this beautiful, bouncy baby isn't just **any** baby ...

... it's your VERY OWN baby brother or sister!